Attending
Minecon

By Josh Gregory

Published in the United States of America by
Cherry Lake Publishing
Ann Arbor, Michigan
www.cherrylakepublishing.com

Reading Adviser: Marla Conn, Read-Ability
Photo Credits: Cover and pages 8 and 12, Kevin Burnett / tinyurl.com/y9a2xugk / CC BY 2.0; page 4, ©Bloomicon/Shutterstock; page 6, ©VanoVasaio/Shutterstock; page 10, ©Pabkov/Shutterstock; page 14, ©Tinxi/Shutterstock; pages 16 and 18, Bo Mertz / tinyurl.com/y748w9z9 / CC BY-SA 2.0; page 20, ©Ga Fullner/Shutterstock.

Library of Congress Cataloging-in-Publication Data has been filed and is available at catalog.loc.gov

Cherry Lake Publishing would like to acknowledge the work of the Partnership for 21st Century Learning. Please visit *www.p21.org* for more information.

Printed in the United States of America
Corporate Graphics

Table of Contents

People play *Minecraft* using tablets, smartphones, game consoles, and PCs.

A Global Community

Millions upon millions of people have journeyed through the world of *Minecraft*. The game's fans live all around the world. They are all ages. They come from different backgrounds and have different interests. But they all have one thing in common. They love playing *Minecraft* and sharing their adventures with each other!

Popular *Minecraft* streamers can draw huge audiences of fans.

Shared Experiences

Fans have gone online to share tips, hints, and other information about *Minecraft* ever since the game was first released in 2009. They play together online. They post on message boards and in chat rooms. They **stream** themselves playing the game so others can watch. But what if they want to share their love of *Minecraft* in person?

Fans go crazy with excitement when famous faces take the stage at Minecon events.

Celebrating Minecraft

Minecon is one of the biggest events on any *Minecraft* fan's calendar each year. It is a **convention**, or con, where *Minecraft* players gather to celebrate their favorite game. Minecon is an official event that is hosted by *Minecraft*'s creators. People come from all around the world to attend!

Minecraft Meetups

Some *Minecraft* fans form clubs or host smaller events of their own. They get together every so often to play multiplayer mode. These events are often hosted at schools and libraries. Check to see if there is one near you!

MinecraftCon 2010 took place in Bellevue, Washington. Only a few people attended.

MinecraftCon 2010

In 2010, *Minecraft* creator Markus "Notch" Persson hosted a very small gathering of fans in Washington State. He jokingly called the event MinecraftCon 2010. *Minecraft* was still a new game. It had a small online community of hard-core fans. But soon it would become more popular than Notch could have guessed.

Each Minecon sells out almost as soon as tickets go on sale! Minecon 2016 in California drew the largest audience of any Minecon.

Bigger and Better

By 2011, *Minecraft* had millions of players all around the world. Notch's company, Mojang, announced the first official Minecon. It was held in Las Vegas, Nevada. Thousands of people flew in from 24 different countries. Since then, Minecon has only gotten bigger. It has been held in several different cities.

A Hot Ticket

Here is a list of how many people attended each live Minecon event:

Year	Location	Attendees
2011	Las Vegas, Nevada	4,500
2012	Paris, France	4,500
2013	Orlando, Florida	7,500
2015	London, England	10,000
2016	Anaheim, California	12,000

*There was no Minecon event in 2014.

One of the most fun parts of Minecon is seeing people dressed in *Minecraft* costumes. Here, a woman pretends to be a Creeper.

Sights and Sounds

There is a lot to see and do at a Minecon event. There are huge *Minecraft* decorations everywhere you look. For example, you might see life-size versions of the game's most fearsome enemies. You might spot fans dressed up as their favorite characters. There are also *Minecraft* toys, shirts, and other fun things for sale.

Minecraft creators such as Jens "Jeb" Bergensten are among the many famous faces at Minecon events.

On Stage

The main events at Minecon take place on stage in packed **auditoriums**. Here, the game's creators talk about what they're working on. They show off footage of new features they plan to add to the game. Sometimes they even take questions from the audience. Famous *Minecraft* streamers sometimes take the stage to entertain fans.

Streamers love to meet their fans face-to-face. Here, a popular streamer signs an autograph for a fan at Minecon 2012.

Meeting Minecraft Heroes

Have you ever wanted to meet your favorite *Minecraft* celebrities? Many popular streamers, **modders**, and other creators attend Minecon. Some of them meet with fans to sign autographs and take pictures. Be prepared, though. Sometimes you have to wait in long lines before you come face-to-face with the biggest *Minecraft* stars.

Actor Will Arnett hosted Minecon Earth 2017. He has starred in many movies and TV series. He is also a big *Minecraft* fan!

The Future of Minecon

In 2017, Mojang introduced a new kind of Minecon called Minecon Earth. This version was not an in-person event. Instead, it was streamed online. The 2018 Minecon was also a Minecon Earth event. But this time, fans were able to attend official Minecon Earth parties around the world. They could hang out, meet *Minecraft* stars, and watch the live stream. It's like a mini-Minecon!

Looking Back

Did you miss last year's Minecon? Or maybe you just want to see your favorite parts again. Either way, you're in luck. Most Minecon events are recorded and **archived** on YouTube. You can watch them anytime!

Glossary

archived (AHR-kivd) stored for later use

auditoriums (aw-dih-TOR-ee-uhmz) large rooms where people gather to watch performances on stage

convention (kuhn-VEN-shuhn) an event where people with shared interests gather together

modders (MAH-durz) people who make unofficial modifications to a video game

stream (STREEM) to broadcast live audio or video over the internet

Find Out More

Books

Milton, Stephanie. *Minecraft Essential Handbook*. New York: Scholastic, 2015.

Milton, Stephanie. *Minecraft: Guide to Exploration*. New York: Del Rey, 2017.

Web Sites

Minecraft—Minecon
https://minecraft.net/en-us/minecon
Check out the official Minecon page for more info on each year's events.

Minecraft Wiki
https://minecraft.gamepedia.com/Minecraft_Wiki
Minecraft's many fans work together to maintain this detailed guide to the game.

Index

About the Author

Josh Gregory is the author of more than 125 books for young readers. He currently lives in Chicago, Illinois.